UNDERSTANDING THE PARANORMAL

Investigating Angels and Demons

DANIELLE WEINER

Britannica
Educational Publishing

IN ASSOCIATION WITH

ROSEN
EDUCATIONAL SERVICES

Published in 2017 by Britannica Educational Publishing (a trademark of Encyclopædia Britannica, Inc.) in association with The Rosen Publishing Group, Inc.
29 East 21st Street, New York, NY 10010

Distributed exclusively by Rosen Publishing.
To see additional Britannica Educational Publishing titles, go to rosenpublishing.com.

First Edition

Britannica Educational Publishing
J.E. Luebering: Executive Director, Core Editorial
Anthony L. Green: Editor, Compton's by Britannica

Rosen Publishing
Jacob R. Steinberg: Editor
Nelson Sá: Art Director
Brian Garvey: Designer
Cindy Reiman: Photography Manager
Karen Huang: Photo Researcher

Library of Congress Cataloging-in-Publication Data

Names: Weiner, Danielle, author.
Title: Investigating angels and demons / Danielle Weiner.
Description: First Edition. | New York : Britannica Educational Publishing,
  2017. | Series: Understanding the paranormal | Includes bibliographical
  references and index.
Identifiers: LCCN 2015045374| ISBN 9781680485714 (library bound : alk. paper)
  | ISBN 9781680485769 (pbk. : alk. paper) | ISBN 9781680485530 (6-pack :
  alk. paper)
Subjects: LCSH: Angels. | Demonology.
Classification: LCC BL477 .W45 2016 | DDC 202/.15—dc23
LC record available at http://lccn.loc.gov/2015045374

Manufactured in the United States of America

CONTENTS

INTRODUCTION 4

CHAPTER 1
WHAT ARE ANGELS
AND DEMONS?. 6

CHAPTER 2
HISTORY OF ANGELS
AND DEMONS 16

CHAPTER 3
ARE SPIRITUAL MESSENGERS
REAL?. 26

CHAPTER 4
ANGELS IN LITERATURE, ART,
AND POPULAR CULTURE 34

GLOSSARY 43

FOR FURTHER READING 45

INDEX 47

INTRODUCTION

Throughout history, humans have sought to understand and order the world. In doing so, they've looked to cosmology, astronomy, and physical science. We are often concerned with boundaries—or what makes us different from other animate beings. Different religions have developed different systems for ordering and dividing the cosmos. The most familiar view—generally found in the Jewish, Christian, and Muslim religions—is one of a universe divided into three parts: heaven, Earth, and hell. This view of the cosmos has influenced the popular concept of angels and demons—the spiritual beings that navigate between Earth and heaven or hell, respectively. (In Eastern, ancient, and nonurban cultures, the division between kind and evil spiritual beings is less strict; they may be kind in some circumstances and evil in others.)

In the Abrahamic religious traditions, angels are said to watch over and help humanity. Some traditions even insist that each individual has his or her own guardian angel to watch over him or her. Angels have their significance primarily in what they do rather than in what they are. They carry out the messages and will of a higher being, generally God. Demons, in turn, lure humans from their spiritual path. Their nature and the source of their authority differ in various traditions. Regardless of religious doctrine or belief, angels and demons have firmly entered the earthly realm; their influence on popular culture has made them a permanent fixture in books, films, and art.

he Angel with the Millstone, *from the Bamberg Apocalypse Illuminated Manuscript, 1000–20, offers a Christian conception of an angel during the Middle Ages.*

CHAPTER ONE

WHAT ARE ANGELS AND DEMONS?

In many religious traditions there exists a concept of spiritual beings commonly known as angels and demons. Angels are generally good, benevolent spirits. The word "angel" is derived from the Greek word *angelos*, meaning "messenger." Although the meaning of the word "angel" points toward their purpose rather than their essence or nature, in most traditions angels are thought to be spirits who perform various services for God or for humans on God's behalf.

Angels have their counterpart in demons, or evil spirits. The word "demon" is derived from the Greek term, *daimon*. Though commonly associated with an evil spirit, the term originally meant a spiritual being that influenced a person's character. However, over

rchangel Gabriel fulfills the traditional role of the angel as messenger when he mounces to the Virgin Mary that she will give birth to Jesus in The Annunciation, *15th-century painting by Fra Angelico.*

time the term came to designate the lesser spirits of the supernatural realm who influenced men to perform negative actions.

ZOROASTRIANISM

Despite the largely Christian influence on how popular culture envisions angels and demons, the origins of belief in these beings can be traced to the ancient

This detail of a 5th- or 6th-century-BCE painting from a Zoroastrian temple in Iran depicts Zoroaster, a Persian religious leader and founder of Zoroastrianism.

Persian religion of Zoroastrianism.

Zoroastrianism is an ancient Iranian religion that was reformed during the 7th and 6th centuries BCE by a legendary figure named Zoroaster. Followers of Zoroaster believed the world was created by Ahura Mazda, meaning "Wise Lord." Ahura Mazda created two supreme beings: Spenta Mainyu, a good spirit, and Ahriman, an evil spirit. World history is defined by the struggle between these two spirits.

In addition to Spenta Mainyu and Ahriman, Zoroastrianism teaches that six angels known as the *amesha spentas* help Ahura Mazda govern the world and battle Ahriman. Each *amesha spenta* is opposed by a *daeva*, a demon that serves Ahriman.

JUDAISM, CHRISTIANITY, AND ISLAM

The three major Abrahamic religions of Judaism, Christianity, and Islam share the belief that there is a class of spiritual beings between God and humans. Angels typically

his detail of Abraham and the Archangel Michael, *from mid-12th-century Lower xony, Germany, depicts the Judeo-Christian archangel Michael.*

serve God as messengers or carry out God's will. Demons typically oppose angels and challenge mankind to sin.

All three major Abrahamic religions have several aspects in common. For instance, all three share certain archangels (angels of a higher order). The four archangels specifically named in the Hebrew Bible are Michael, the leader of the angels; Gabriel, God's messenger; Raphael, a healer; and Uriel, the watcher over the world and the lowest part of hell. They also share belief in seraphim and cherubim. These winged beings serve as throne guardians for God.

Also common to the three major Abrahamic religions is the figure known as Satan, or the devil. Each religion has distinct interpretations of Satan and his role.

SATAN

The Hebrew term *satan* means "adversary." It is used in the Hebrew Bible as a title to refer to any opponent or enemy, without supernatural connotations. The idea of a singular evil being named Satan would develop in Christianity.

In the New Testament, Satan is spoken of as the prince of evil spirits. He is also identified with the term "devil." He is the enemy of God and of Christ and takes the guise of an angel of light. In Christian theology the devil's main task is to tempt man to reject the way of salvation and to accept the path of destruction. He can enter a man and act through him. According to the visions in the Book of Revelation, when Christ returns from heaven to reign on earth, Satan will face final defeat and be cast into eternal punishment.

The Islamic equivalent of Satan is called Iblis. At the time of the creation of humans, God ordered his angels to bow down before Adam, the first man. Iblis refused, claiming that he was a nobler being. For this display

The Devil Presenting St. Augustine with the Book of Vices, by Michael Pacher, c. 1455–1498, is an illustration of the Devil or Satan as he is perceived in Christianity.

of pride, God cast Iblis out of heaven. Iblis's punishment, however, is postponed until the Judgment Day, when he and his host will have to face the eternal fires of hell. Until that time he is allowed to tempt all but true believers to evil. Iblis is also called the "enemy of God," "enemy," or when he is portrayed as a tempter, *ash-Shaytan* ("demon").

CHRISTIANITY

In the New Testament, angels are present at all important events in the life of Jesus, from his birth to the Resurrection. In the very dramatic Book of Revelation, angels are portrayed as the agents of God in bringing judgment upon the world. St. Paul takes note of angels by assigning them ranks. He lists seven groups: angels, archangels, principalities, powers, virtues, dominions, and thrones. The Old Testament had spoken of only two orders: cherubim and seraphim.

Early Christianity accepted all nine ranks and in the course of time developed extensive doctrines about angels and demons. The main function of angels is to praise and serve God and to do his will. Angels are thought to reveal divine truths and to help humans gain salvation or special

Twelfth-century frescoes from the crypt of Monte Maria Abbey in Trentino-Alto Adige, Italy, present this painting of a six-winged seraph, an angel commonly depicted based on its description in the vision of the prophet Isaiah.

graces or favors. Guardian angels are believed to watch over individuals and nations. The view that there are guardian angels watching over children has been significant in the popular belief of Roman Catholics. Angels are also thought to lead the souls of the dead to the afterlife.

ANGELS AND DEMONS IN EASTERN RELIGIONS

Belief in supernatural spirits has not been limited to the major Western religions. In Eastern religions such as Hinduism, Jainism, and Buddhism, there is generally no belief in angels. Instead, the function of angels is carried by spiritual beings such as *avataras* and *boddhisattvas*, who are considered extensions of God or the sacred. Belief in demons, however, is widespread. Hinduism has many demons, called *asuras*, who oppose the *devas* (gods). In Buddhism demons are seen as tempters who prevent the achievement of nirvana. In indigenous Chinese religions, after a person's death, the soul becomes either of two spirits: the *shen*, which ascends to the spirit world, or the *guei*, a demon, which remains within the grave. Among the most fearsome of the Japanese demons are the *oni*, evil spirits with much power, and the *tengu*, spirits that possess humans.

Demons are fallen angels. They are conceived of as Satan's legions, sent out to lure humankind away from belief in God. Medieval Christian scholars would create corresponding ranks to match demons to St. Paul's angelic ranks. Besides tempting humans to sin, demons were believed to cause various types of misfortunes, both natural and accidental.

ISLAM

In Islam angels and demons play similar roles as in Judaism and Christianity. These spirits are often mentioned in the Islamic holy book, the Koran.

Furthermore, a lower order of supernatural beings called jinn, or genies, exists. These are beings that may be either good or evil spirits. They are below the level of

A 17th-century illustration from Mughal India of Islamic jinn, also translated as "genies," depicted with animal heads.

angels and devils. Jinn are said to be capable of taking human or animal form, as well as dwelling in natural objects. They are said to be responsible for diseases and accidents and generally cause trouble for human beings.

Two specific classes of jinn are the *ghuls* and the *silas*. Ghuls could change form. They were said to stalk the desert, often in the guise of an attractive woman, trying to distract travelers, and, when successful, kill and eat them. The sila was a witchlike species of jinn that could not change shape.

CHAPTER TWO

HISTORY OF ANGELS AND DEMONS

The Zoroastrian concept of angels as agents of a supreme deity first emerged in about 1000 BCE. Many scholars believe Judaism first had contact with elements of Zoroastrian belief in angels and demons during the Babylonian Exile (598–538 BCE), when Jews were held captive in Babylonia, and during subsequent Persian rule (539–330 BCE). From Judaism, these concepts later carried over to Christianity and Islam. Nonetheless, angels and demons were not entirely a Zoroastrian import; spiritual messengers that served God were present in portions of the Hebrew Bible that predate the Babylonian Exile.

is detail of a relief from the palace of the Assyrian king Sargon II, from the 7th
ntury BCE, depicts a winged genie as it was portrayed in Assyrian culture. Assyrian
iefs influenced Judaism during the Babylonian Exile and later Persian rule.

IN JUDAISM

Several works of early Jewish literature would significantly develop Jewish ideas about angels and demons. One of the most important of these works is the Talmud, a commentary on, and supplement to, the written law of the Hebrew Bible. Compiled between the 2nd and 6th centuries CE, the Talmud significantly developed the Judaic concept of angels and demons. It included distinctions between good

DYBBUKS

In the 16th century, Jewish mysticism (known as Kabbala) developed the concept of two categories of spiritual beings closely resembling the Christian concepts of angels and demons. The evil being is the *dybbuk*, a wandering human spirit that restlessly seeks the body of a living person to occupy. Jewish folklore spread the belief that a person could be possessed by a dybbuk and that dybbuks were the source of nervous or mental disorders. Such patients could consult miracle-working rabbis, who would remove the dybbuk from a living person through a religious rite of exorcism. The counterpart to the dybbuk is the *ibbur*. An ibbur is the benevolent spirit of a departed being that returns after its death to perform positive deeds while occupying living humans.

angels and evil angels and added thoughts on the nature of angels previously unseen in Judaism.

IN CHRISTIANITY

As Christianity developed from Judaism in the 1st century CE, early Christian beliefs and practices often resembled those of Judaism. Christianity inherited Judaism's principal angels, including its archangels. Throughout Late Antiquity angels acquired specific characteristics, both in art and theology.

In the Middle Ages, there was an increase in the systematic study of angels and demons in Christianity. Christian philosophers—notably St. Thomas Aquinas (b. c. 1225–d. 1274)—wrote extensively on angels, categorizing and organizing them. Some medieval scholars

e Apotheosis of St. Thomas Aquinas, m the altarpiece by Francesco Traini, 3, presents St. Thomas Aquinas.

assigned seven archdemons to the seven deadly sins: Lucifer (Pride); Mammon (Avarice); Asmodeus (Lechery); Satan (Anger); Beelzebub (Gluttony); Leviathan (Envy); and Belphegor (Sloth). In the Middle Ages, demons came to be viewed as the agents of famine, disease, war, earthquakes, accidental deaths, and mental or emotional disorders.

ANGELS IN ISLAM

With the emergence and spread of Islam in the 7th century CE, we may begin to speak of a strictly Islamic interpretation of angels and demons. Islam incorporated the angels of Judaism and Christianity. Therefore, angels in Islam have a similar role: they are messengers between heaven and Earth. According to Islam, it was the archangel Gabriel who appeared to the Prophet Muhammad and revealed to him the Koran, Islam's holy text.

Unlike humans and the mischievous jinn, angels are not contained to the physical world. The Koran does not mention the creation of angels, and it hardly refers to angels by individual names. The archangels Gabriel and Michael appear as messengers of God, however neither is called an "angel." When angels are mentioned in the

Koran, the term used is *malak*, which shares roots with the Hebrew word *malakh*. Accounts of angels in the Koran refer to the same angels who exist in the Hebrew Bible, with similar stories and characteristics.

...hammad and the Archangel Gabriel, ...n the Siyer-i Nebi, *a Turkish epic ...tten in 1388 and illustrated in 1595, ...sents a Muslim depiction of the ...hangel Gabriel.*

In the West, the concept of angels and demons lost importance following the Copernican revolution in the 16th century. Copernicus's teachings that the Earth was not the center of the cosmos, but rather, one of many planets revolving around the Sun changed religious beliefs about the cosmos: heaven above, hell

Hieronymus Bosch's 15th-century painting titled **The Garden of Earthly Delights** *portrays a three-part universe, consisting of heaven (left), hell (right), and Earth in between.*

below, and Earth in between. Angels and demons, the supposed intermediaries between these realms, no longer had a place in science's worldview.

With the emergence of modern Western psychology in the 19th and 20th centuries, however, the underlying principles of beliefs in angels and demons took on new meanings. Many Christian theologians found concepts of psychoanalysis helpful in reinterpreting the meanings underlying traditional beliefs in angels and demons. Carl Jung, a Swiss psychologist and psychiatrist, explained belief in angels and demons as a deep psychological pattern; he suggested that angels and demons were personified aspects of the human unconscious, rather than literal spiritual beings.

REEMERGENCE OF POPULAR BELIEF IN ANGELS

The popular belief in angels as literal beings returned to modern Christian thought in part through the rise of the Evangelical Protestantism movement. The word "evangelism" is derived from a Greek term meaning "good news." Evangelism thus means getting the good news out or spreading the word (in this case, the teachings of Jesus). Since the late 1800s mass evangelism has been associated with certain dynamic preachers, notably Dwight L. Moody, Billy Sunday, Aimee Semple McPherson, and Billy Graham.

In the 1940s, a Christian evangelist named Billy Graham started to conduct preaching campaigns in an entertaining style. He had a popular radio program, *Hour of Decision*, and quickly became well known around the world. In 1975, Graham wrote a book called

Popular evangelist Billy Graham pictured on the set of a television broadcast on July 24, 1962, in Los Angeles, California.

Angels: God's Secret Agents that investigated the nature and purpose of angels in the Bible. The book was successful and inspired others to write books that explored the biblical study of angels. Novelists picked up on the new trend and began to write Christian fiction about the worldly struggle between angels and demons.

Parallel to the reemergence of an interest in angelology in Christianity, other movements throughout the 19th and 20th centuries embraced the idea of supernatural spiritual beings similar to angels. Such movements include spiritualism (a 19th-century movement based on the belief that the living can contact the dead), the Theosophical Society (a mystical group whose doctrine included the belief in a spiritual reality—which may be called God—that people may experience through meditation, revelation, intuition, or some other state that takes the individual beyond a normal consciousness), and the New Age movement (a movement that spread through the occult and metaphysical religious communities in the 1970s and '80s and preached the arrival of a "New Age" of human awareness).

Though they emerge from established traditions, the New Age context casts angels not as messengers or servers of God, but as servers of people. They are seen as compassionate, kind, nonjudgmental, and a readily available source for human inspiration and spiritual connection. Theosophical and New Age groups claim the ability to receive channeled messages from various supernatural beings through such actions as yoga, meditation, tarot card reading, and crystal ball reading.

CHAPTER THREE

ARE SPIRITUAL MESSENGERS REAL?

A fter the Enlightenment and the scientific revolution, a new era began in the Western world that persists to this day. In explaining the natural world, science is valued over religion, and rational explanations over the supernatural.

Nevertheless, strict believers of religious traditions and members of various New Age movements have tried to reconcile traditional religious descriptions of angels and demons with science. Such attempts to prove the existence of angels and demons rely on unconventional interpretations of the spiritual beings.

QUANTUM EXPLANATIONS?

After a period of conflict between science and religion in the 19th and 20th centuries, the rise of New Age movements has led to attempts to reconcile religion and science. Included in these attempts has been a re-examination of the concept of angels. Adherents of New Age movements often look to quantum physics to re-examine commonly held beliefs about the way the physical world operates.

QUANTUM PHYSICS

Quantum physics is the study of matter on the atomic and subatomic scale. It accounts for the properties and actions of molecules, atoms, and their smaller constituents. Quantum physics has revealed that matter and radiation at extremely small scales act differently than at the larger, familiar scales of the everyday world, described by classical physics. At the small scales that quantum physics studies, behavior of matter can seem unusual or strange.

Max Planck, the German theoretical physicist who originated quantum theory (for which he won the Nobel Prize for physics in 1918), is photographed in 1933 in Germany.

In 1996 American theologian Matthew Fox and English biologist Rupert Sheldrake published *The Physics of Angels*. The pair closely examined St. Thomas Aquinas's description of angels as invisible beings without mass or body. Sheldrake writes, "Angels are quantized...They move as units of action. The only way you can detect their presence is through action; they are quanta of action." He goes on to equate this description of angels with Albert Einstein's description of photons, or light quanta. He says, "Angels, according to Aquinas, have no mass, they have no body. And the same goes for photons: they are massless, and you can detect them only by their action."

Attempts have been made to use other concepts in quantum physics to explain spiritual phenomena. For instance, a concept known as quantum entanglement (or as Einstein called it, "spooky action at a distance") describes "the idea that two physically separated particles can have correlated properties." In November 2015 researchers at the National Institute of Standards and Technology conducted experiments that seemed to support the possibility that two discrete photons sent to different locations could affect each other's measurement.

New Age believers cite such experiments to support the idea that information (or divine influence) can affect actions at a distance. Most physicists do not take seriously such correlations between quantum entanglement and "angelic" influences. The field dedicated to

Photon filters, such as the one shown here, are used in quantum entanglement experiments to explore how two quanta affect each other at a distance. This experiment was performed at the University of Geneva in February 2003.

correlating quantum physics with spiritual, New Age principles is (often mockingly) called "quantum mysticism."

IT'S ALL IN YOUR MIND

Developments in the field of psychology in the late 19th and early 20th centuries led to new theories to explain parapsychological experiences (events that cannot be accounted for by natural law or knowledge). Some skeptics claim the witnessing of paranormal beings (such as angels or demons) is the result of psychological disorders or irregular brain activity.

Neurologists know that stimulation of certain parts of the brain can cause the mind to play tricks on itself and conjure up images, false memories, and hallucinations. Hyperactivity in a certain part of the brain called the temporoparietal junction can cause illusions, hallucinations of beings present besides the self, and feelings of paranoia. These symptoms are commonly associated with schizophrenia, a mental disorder. Some psychologists have tried to explain visions of angels and supernatural beings as the result of stimulation of or irregular activity in parts of the brain responsible for distinction between the self and other.

A SOCIAL THEORY

Belief or experience with angels may also be socially conditioned. Parapsychology relies on three types of evidence to explore unexplainable phenomena: controlled experimental evidence in laboratories, recurring spontaneous evidence that can be scientifically investigated, and anecdotal evidence, or stories from people who claim to have had a supernatural experience. Anecdotal evidence is among the most widespread—and least scientifically trustworthy—form of evidence.

Some sociologists have suggested that accounts of interactions with angels and divine beings are shaped by

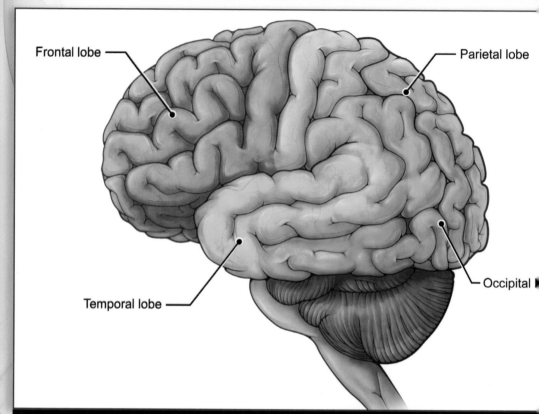

Frontal lobe

Parietal lobe

Temporal lobe

Occipital

An illustration of the human brain notes the four lobes of the brain. Some scientists believe that hallucinations of spiritual beings may be caused by hyperactivity where the temporal and parietal lobes meet.

religious and cultural norms—that is, they reflect existing notions of what an encounter with a divine being must be. Certain experiences that an individual cannot fully understand may be easily understood as the influence of angels or demons. Parapsychological experiences are understood through the cultural, religious, and educational background of the individual having the experience. Therefore, a highly religious or spiritual individual is more likely to interpret a vision caused by irregular mental activity as an encounter with a particular religious figure or an angel.

Scientific examination of experiences with angels or demons can lead to heated debates. Discussion about parapsychological phenomena has sometimes assumed emotional overtones, unsuitable to scientific discipline. Believers and nonbelievers are often biased in their examination of phenomena. When such extreme and contradictory views are widely held, it is difficult to reach a definite conclusion on the existence of spiritual beings.

CHAPTER FOUR

ANGELS IN LITERATURE, ART, AND POPULAR CULTURE

Fascination with angels and demons (especially the Devil) has led to their frequent depiction in works of art and literature, throughout history and today. The paintings, stained glass, mosaics, and sculptures of the Middle Ages and Renaissance are especially replete with figures of angels and demons.

IN LITERATURE

In John Milton's long poem *Paradise Lost* (1667), Satan himself is a main character. The angels Raphael,

Gabriel, and Michael play prominent roles. The poem tells the biblical story of the fall from grace of Adam and Eve. Milton portrays Satan in a sympathetic way, which some literary scholars have argued casts him as the hero of the story, though his goal is to corrupt mankind. Though he is head of the rebellious angels, Satan's quest to overthrow God is unsuccessful and lands him in hell.

In Dante's long narrative poem *The Divine Comedy* (1321), angels appear as both messengers and guardians. Satan is vividly

Satan, or the Devil, as envisioned by Gustave Doré in his illustrations of John Milton's epic poem Paradise Lost *(1667).*

portrayed frozen in a block of ice. The text narrates a miraculous visit to Hell, Purgatory, and Paradise by a visitor, whose name is also Dante.

This illustration of the Devil, known as Mephistopheles in the Faust legends by Johann Wolfgang von Goethe, depicts him with Faust, as illustrated by A. Jacomin, 1869.

The 16th-century legendary magician Faust owes his first literary fame to the anonymous author of *Das Faustbuch* (*The Faust Book*), published in Frankfurt am Main in 1587. The book was a collection of tales concerning a number of ancient and medieval magicians, wizards, and sorcerers who had gone by the name of Faust. The book relates how Faust sought to acquire supernatural knowledge and power by a bargain with Satan. In this pact, signed with his own blood, Faust agreed that Mephistopheles, a devil, was to become his servant for 24 years. In return, Faust would surrender himself to Satan. Mephistopheles entertained his master with luxurious living, long intellectual conversations, and with glimpses of the spirit world. After the agreed to 24 years, during an earthquake, Faust was carried off to hell.

Contemporary young adult fiction often draws on paranormal phenomena to create thrilling science-fiction-fueled teen dramas. In Lauren Kate's *Fallen* (2009), the main character, Luce, attends a boarding

ANGELS IN ART

Some religious traditions, particularly Islam, are iconoclastic, meaning they do not often represent figures in their art. Therefore, Christian art has more heavily influenced imagery of angels and demons. Images of angels and demons appear in visual art as early as the 2nd century ce. Before the 5th century, angels in Christian art were depicted as wingless. Some of the earliest forms of illustrations were published in illuminated manuscripts (illustrated religious texts).

The image of the winged human as angel emerged in the Christian art of the 15th-century Byzantine period. Angels and divine figures were often depicted in human form with halos. One of the first well-known paintings that depicts angels in human form is Andrey Rublyov's *The Old Testament Trinity* (c. 1410). The subject is the biblical

Andrey Rublyov's The Old Testament Trinity *(c. 1410) depicts divine figures in human form.*

story of the visit of three angels to Abraham and Sarah. The angels are portrayed as clothed human figures with golden halos and wings; Abraham and Sarah are not pictured.

Over time images of angels became increasingly human-like. During the Renaissance angels were portrayed as existing within the same realm as humans. In Fra Angelico's Annalena Altarpiece (c. 1438), two angels occupy the same physical space as the Madonna and Christ Child, and appear to be in conversation. It is the Renaissance images of angels that have most influenced popular imagery of angels as winged human beings.

school of students who are secretly fallen angels. Some students are on the side of God and others are on the side of Satan. The characters are presented as eclectic and possess supernatural powers, such as superhuman strength. While biblical references are present in the series, the actions of the angels are fictionalized.

Also popular is a genre of Christian fiction that draws on real religious belief in angels and demons. American author Frank E. Peretti was highly successful in crafting this genre in the 1980s. His novel *This Present Darkness* (1986) presented a contemporary view on angels and demons engaged in the struggle to control a small American town.

FILM AND TELEVISION

In film and television, angels have been depicted in a variety of manners. Some approaches are faithful to religious teachings, while others focus on the power of angels to communicate messages or perform superhuman acts.

Perhaps the most famous film of the holiday season is Frank Capra's *It's a Wonderful Life* (1946), a story about a small-town man, George Bailey (played by James Stewart), who thinks himself a failure until his guardian angel, Clarence (Henry Travers), appears on Christmas

Eve to show him the value of his life. Clarence and George Bailey became two of the most well-known characters in film history. One of the best-known television

A 1999 photograph of the cast of the television series Touched by an Angel, *a popular series that ran from 1994 to 2003.*

series in the United States, *Touched by an Angel* (1994–2003), depicted angels dispatched from heaven to provide guidance to people at crossroads in their lives. The show largely centered on Monica, one of the guardian angels. The show also depicted the Angel of Death, who helped Monica with her cases. The show had a religious undertone, as Monica brought messages of hope from God to individuals and learned lessons of her own. The angels were depicted in human form.

The Devil has received a variety of treatments in visual media. The 1973 film *The Exorcist*, based on William Peter Blatty's best-selling novel of the same name, is a frightening tale of the supernatural that focuses on a young girl who is believed to be possessed by the Devil. Although the center of much controversy when released in 1973, it became one of the highest-grossing films of all time and earned 10 Academy Award nominations. In the popular 1997 mystery thriller *The Devil's Advocate*, Al Pacino plays Satan in the form of the morally corrupt head of a New York City law firm. Such an approach is popular. In 2016 the television show *Lucifer* portrayed the Devil in human form as a Los Angeles club owner whom the police consult in pursuit of criminals. Other depictions stuck to the iconic horned red figure. Notable is *Legend* (1985), a fantasy film in which Tim Curry depicts the "Lord of Darkness."

A photograph of actor Tim Curry as the Devil in the film Legend *(1985).*

The representations of angels and demons in popular culture reflect the diverse views of angels and demons in different traditions. While science has diminished belief in such beings, the persistence of the notion of angels and demons says much about the nature of humankind. Even the most rational among us may have a need to feel guided and protected, at times. Angels serve such a purpose.

GLOSSARY

ABRAHAMIC Referring to those religions that revere the biblical Abraham as a patriarch, namely Judaism, Christianity, and Islam.

ANGELOLOGY The religious doctrine of angels or its study.

CHERUB A type of angel that is usually shown in art as a beautiful young child with small wings and a round face and body.

ILLUMINATED MANUSCRIPT A handwritten book decorated with gold or silver, brilliant colors, or elaborate designs or miniature pictures.

MIDDLE AGES The period of European history from about 500 to about 1500 CE.

MYSTICISM The experience of mystical union or direct communication with God or a divine force.

NEW AGE Of or relating to an eclectic group of cultural attitudes arising in late 20th-century Western society that are adapted from those of a variety of cultures ancient and modern, that emphasize beliefs (as reincarnation, holism, pantheism, and occultism) outside the mainstream, and that advance alternative approaches to spirituality, right living, and health.

NIRVANA The state of perfect happiness and peace in Buddhism where there is release from all forms of suffering.

PARANOIA A serious mental disorder marked especially by feelings of persecution or an exaggerated sense of one's own importance, usually without hallucinations.

PARAPSYCHOLOGY The study of events that cannot be explained by what scientists know about nature and the world.

RENAISSANCE The period of European history between the 14th and 17th centuries marked by a flourishing of art and literature inspired by ancient times and by the beginnings of modern science.

SERAPH One of the six-winged angels standing in the presence of God.

SPIRITUALISM A belief that the spirits of the dead communicate with the living.

QUANTUM PHYSICS A branch of physics that deals with the structure and behavior of very small pieces of matter.

THEOLOGY A system of religious beliefs or ideas.

THEOSOPHICAL Of or related to the teachings of a modern movement (The Theosophical Society) originating in the United States in 1875 and following chiefly Buddhist and Brahmanic theories of evolution and reincarnation.

FOR FURTHER READING

Albert Jones, David. *Angels, A History*. New York, NY: Oxford University Press, 2010.

Alexander, Audrey. *Angels, Demons, and Religious Rituals*. Pittsburgh, PA: Eldorado Ink, 2015.

Fox, Matthew, and Rupert Sheldrake. *The Physics of Angels: Exploring the Realm Where Science and Spirit Meet*. New York, NY: Monkfish Book Publishing, 2014.

Guiley, Rosemary Ellen. *The Encyclopedia of Angels*. 2nd ed. New York, NY: Facts On File, Inc. 2004.

Henneberg, Susan. *Investigating Ghosts and the Spirit World*. New York, NY: Britannica Educational Publishing, 2015.

Jaritz, Gerhard. *Angels, Devils: The Supernatural and Its Visual Representation*. Budapest, Hungary: Central European University Press, 2011.

Keck, David. *Angels and Angelology in the Middle Ages*. New York, NY: Oxford University Press, 1998.

Lewis, James R., and Evelyn Dorothy Oliver. *Angels A to Z*. Michigan: Visible Ink Press, 2008.

Llewellyn, Claire. *Saints and Angels*. London, England: Kingfisher, 2013.

Steinberg, Lewis M. *Investigating Miracles*. New York, NY: Britannica Educational Publishing, 2016.

Tart, Charles T. *Body, Mind, Spirit: Exploring the Parapsychology of Spirituality*. Virginia: Hampton Roads Publishing Company, 1997.

WEBSITES

Because of the changing nature of Internet links, Rosen Publishing has developed an online list of websites related to the subject of this book. This site is updated regularly. Please use this link to access this list:

http://www.rosenlinks.com/UTP/angel

INDEX

A

Ahriman, 8
Ahura Mazda, 8
amesha spentas, 8
Angels: God's Secret Agents, 24
Annalena Altarpiece, 38
art, 5, 19, 34, 37–38
ash-Shaytan, 11
Asmodeus, 20
asuras, 13
avataras, 13

B

Beelzebub, 20
Belphegor, 20
boddhisattvas, 13
Buddhism, 13

C

cherubim, 10

Christianity, 4, 7, 10–13, 14, 16, 19–24, 37, 39

D

daeva, 8
devas, 13

E

Evangelical Protestantism, 23

F

films, 5, 39–40, 41

G

ghuls, 15
guei, 13

H

Hinduism, 13

I

ibbur, 18
Iblis, 11
Islam, 4, 9, 10, 11, 14–15, 16,
    20–21

J

Jainism, 13
jinn, 14–15, 20
Judaism, 4, 9, 10, 14, 16,
    18–19, 20
Judgment Day, 11
Jung, Carl, 23

L

literature, 5, 34–37, 39
Lucifer, 20

M

malak, 21
Mammon, 20
Mephistopheles, 36

N

New Age movement, 25, 26,
    27–30

O

*Old Testament Trinity,
    The*, 37–38

oni, 13

P

parapsychology, 30–33

Q

quantum physics, 27–30

R

Raphael, 10, 34
Rubylov, Andrey, 37

S

shen, 13
silas, 15
Spenta Mainyu, 8
spiritualism, 24

T

television, 40–41
tengu, 13
Theosophical Society, 24, 25

Z

Zoroastrianism, 8, 16